Philip Law is Publishing Director at SPCK. His previous books include *A Time to Pray* (Lion, 2002), *The Story of the Christ* (Continuum, 2006) and *The SPCK Book of Christian Prayer* (SPCK, 2009).

D0550954

No time to read the Bible?
Here's an easy way to get started

THE

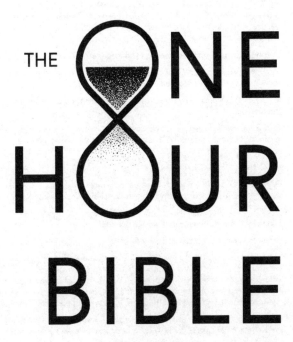

ONE
HOUR
BIBLE

**From Adam to Apocalypse
in sixty minutes**

Edited by
Philip Law

from the text of the
New Living Translation

First published in Great Britain in 2018

Society for Promoting Christian Knowledge
36 Causton Street
London SW1P 4ST
www.spck.org.uk

British Library Cataloguing-in-Publication Data
A catalogue record for this book is available from the British Library

ISBN 978–0–281–07964–3
eBook ISBN 978–0–281–07965–0

Typeset by Colin Hall, www.refinedpractice.com
First printed in Great Britain by Jellyfish Print Solutions
Subsequently digitally printed in Great Britain

eBook by Colin Hall, www.refinedpractice.com

Produced on paper from sustainable forests

Contents

Contents

A note to readers

The *Holy Bible*, New Living Translation, was first published in 1996. It quickly became one of the most popular Bible translations in the English-speaking world. While the NLT's influence was rapidly growing, the Bible Translation Committee determined that an additional investment in scholarly review and text refinement could make it even better. So shortly after its initial publication, the committee began an eight-year process with the purpose of increasing the level of the NLT's precision without sacrificing its easy-to-understand quality. This second-generation text was completed in 2004, with minor changes subsequently introduced in 2007, 2013 and 2015.

The goal of any Bible translation is to convey the meaning and content of the ancient Hebrew, Aramaic and Greek texts as accurately as possible to contemporary readers. The challenge for our translators was to create a text that would communicate as clearly and powerfully to today's readers as the original texts did to readers and listeners in the ancient biblical world. The resulting translation is easy to read and understand, while also accurately communicating the meaning and content of the original biblical texts. The NLT is a general-purpose text especially good for study, devotional reading, and reading aloud in worship services.

Editor's introduction

The Bible is the world's bestselling book. Full of memorable stories, inspiring poetry and timeless wisdom, it has influenced the lives of billions around the world and across the centuries. Yet even those who read it every day will readily admit that it's not always an easy read, and few people manage to read it all the way through.

Why is that? Well, for a start the Bible is very long: most versions of it contain at least 770,000 words – roughly 600,000 in the first section, known as the 'Old Testament', and 170,000 in the second section, or 'New Testament'. (Those figures apply just to the Protestant Bible; the official Roman Catholic and Orthodox Bibles are even longer.)

But as well as finding it very long, if you're new to the Bible you'll soon discover that its contents are just too complex to read comfortably from cover to cover. There are long lists of names, collections of laws, regulations for worship and detailed building instructions; there are histories, chronologies, poems, prayers, proverbs, parables, prophecies and visions; there are Gospels, letters, memoirs, theological reflections, speeches, hymns, and a mysterious form of writing known as 'apocalyptic'.

All these different writings were collected and edited by a range of authors – priests, prophets, poets, sages, apostles – over more than a thousand years. The earliest parts of the 39 books that make up the Old Testament were probably written around three thousand years ago, while the 27 books in the New Testament were probably completed by the end of the first century AD.

Because of this huge diversity, many people prefer to follow a gradual, step-by-step approach to the Bible, taking a few passages at a time and spreading their reading over several months or years. But the disadvantage of that approach is that you can easily end up losing sight of the wood because you're too busy studying the trees! You can end up with a view that's fragmented, disjointed, lacking a sense of how different people, places and events fit together into the bigger picture.

That's where *The One Hour Bible* comes in. Whatever your present level of acquaintance with the Bible, this little book will enable you to stand back and view the epic sweep of the Bible's entire narrative arc – from the majestic opening of the book of Genesis to the final stirring words of Revelation.

In roughly an hour (give or take a few minutes, depending on the speed at which you choose to read it), you will journey along the highways and some of the byways of the Bible's grand narrative. And on the way you'll encounter some of the Bible's most powerful and enduring teachings – including quotations from the spiritual wisdom of Jesus, preserved for us in the Gospels.

What's in *The One Hour Bible*?

Just like the Bible itself, *The One Hour Bible* opens with the dramatic account of Creation in Genesis chapter 1. It goes on to tell of Adam and Eve in the Garden of Eden, their two sons Cain and Abel, then Noah and the Flood and the building of the Tower of Babel.

Next you'll read about the ancestors of the Jews – Abraham, Isaac and Jacob – and how God promises that through them and their descendants he will bless the entire world.

The story of Joseph and his brothers comes next, and then the story of Moses and the Exodus – that crucial turning-point, when God saves his people from their slavery in Egypt. It's at this point that God adopts the Israelites as his 'holy nation', giving them the Ten Commandments and other laws to guide their way.

The story continues with Joshua, the battle of Jericho and the conquest of the Promised Land, leading to the time when the Israelites are ruled by tribal chieftains known as 'judges'.

This leads to the time of Samuel, Saul and David. David is the first great leader to get a firm grip on the Israelite tribes and forge them into a single nation with its capital in Jerusalem. You'll read here of David's triumphs, including the slaying of Goliath. You'll read also of his sins and failures, which include adultery and murder.

The next chapter tells of the legendary wisdom of David's son, King Solomon, famous also for building the first temple in Jerusalem. The golden age of David and

Solomon then ends when the kingdom is torn apart by a rebellion that creates two smaller kingdoms – Israel in the north and Judah in the south.

There then follows a sequence of good kings and bad kings, until the focus is turned on Israel's King Ahab and his consort, the wily Queen Jezebel. Together they conspire to corrupt the nation and lead the people in the worship of foreign gods.

This is the beginning of the period when God sends a series of prophets to warn the people of the disaster that will befall them if they continue to worship idols and disobey God's laws.

But the people, or most of them, refuse to listen. So eventually disaster descends on them in the form of invasions by the armies of Assyria and Babylon, resulting in the total destruction of the kingdom of Israel and the enforced exile of most of the people of Judah.

Hope is rekindled, however, when those empires are in turn replaced by the more enlightened empire of Persia – when Jewish captives like Daniel rise to high office, and the Jews are at last allowed to return to their homeland to begin the task of rebuilding their temple and their nation.

And that's where we leave the fortunes of ancient Israel and Judah, for that's where the Old Testament ends its story.

We then jump a few centuries to the time of Jesus; that is, to the first century of the Christian era. At this point you'll notice that the pace slows down. There are four chapters in *The One Hour Bible* devoted to the life and teaching of Jesus, which accounts for about 20 per cent of the whole text (roughly 12–15 minutes).

The reason for this is that, for Christians, here is the focal point of the entire biblical story – the world-changing moment when God fully reveals his identity in the life of one man, Jesus of Nazareth.

The story of the initial impact of Jesus and his message – the gospel, or 'good news' – comes to us through the New Testament book called the Acts of the Apostles. Here you'll read about the origins of the worldwide Christian faith, beginning on the Day of Pentecost and including some of the great speeches of the Church's first leaders: St Peter in Jerusalem and St Paul in Athens.

Finally, your journey comes to a dazzling end with a few brief extracts from the visions of St John in the book of Revelation – or, as it's sometimes called, the Apocalypse.

What's not in *The One Hour Bible*?

To keep the narrative flowing as smoothly as possible, and to keep the time it takes to read it to about an hour, I've had to leave out a large amount of text. Not only could other prose passages have been included, there's also the beautiful poetry of the book of Job, the Psalms and the Song of Songs – not to mention the wise sayings of Proverbs and Ecclesiastes, the oracles of Isaiah, Jeremiah and Ezekiel, and the inspiring letters that Paul wrote to the early Christians.

None of the parts I've left out, I hasten to add, should be thought of as any less important than those I've included. Many of them contain teachings that are vital for the

Christian faith, especially the letters that make up much of the New Testament.

Having said that, I'm sure there will be some readers who will wonder why I've included some bits rather than others – especially when it comes to the chapters on Jesus. Those chapters were especially challenging; so in choosing what to include I decided to look for passages in the Gospels that most biblical scholars would say display elements that are especially distinctive of Jesus.

Those elements include his emphasis on the need for love to guide our relationships; his concern for the poor, the diseased and disabled; his readiness to eat and mix with social outcasts; his relaxed attitude to Jewish food laws; and his genius for teaching in parables.

What makes *The One Hour Bible* different?

The book you're holding isn't simply another summary or retelling of the Bible. That's been done many times before, both for children and adults. What makes *The One Hour Bible* different is that it's compiled entirely from the text of the Bible itself, using the words of the *Holy Bible*, New Living Translation (see under 'Further reading' at the back of the book).

As well as selecting and arranging the stories, this compilation process has involved radically condensing dozens of passages so as to fit as many as possible into the space available. To give you just one example, the first chapter of the Bible, Genesis 1, has been reduced from 775 words to 123 – a reduction of about 84 per cent.

It's true that some of the depth and texture of the text has been lost in this process. But the aim of this book is to give you the essentials and set them out in a way that helps you to trace the thread of the Bible's overall narrative as it twists and turns through the centuries, and as one generation gives way to another.

There's much more I could add, but I'll end now by saying that I hope you'll enjoy *The One Hour Bible* and that you'll find the stories it contains both entertaining and enlightening. I also hope you'll feel moved to read more of those stories as they appear in the Bible itself. For, like all great stories, those in the Bible aren't just enjoyable and informative. As many people have found, they can even change your life.

Philip Law

PART 1

SCENES FROM THE OLD TESTAMENT

Prologue: In the beginning

In the beginning God created the heavens and the earth. The earth was formless and empty, and darkness covered the deep waters. And the Spirit of God was hovering over the surface.

God said, 'Let there be light,' and there was light.

Then God said, 'Let dry ground appear, and let the land sprout with vegetation. Let the waters swarm with fish. Let the skies be filled with birds. And let the earth produce every sort of animal.' And that is what happened.

Then God said, 'Let us make human beings in our image.' So God created human beings; male and female he created them. Then God looked over all he had made, and saw that it was very good!

So he rested.

1

From Eden to Babel

When God made the earth, God formed man from the dust of the ground. Then God planted a garden in Eden. In the middle he placed the tree of life and the tree of the knowledge of good and evil. A river flowed from the land of Eden, watering the garden.

God placed the man in the garden, but warned him, 'You may freely eat the fruit of every tree – except the tree of the knowledge of good and evil. If you eat its fruit, you are sure to die.'

Then God caused the man to fall into a deep sleep. While the man slept, God took out one of the man's ribs. God made a woman from the rib and brought her to the man. The man and his wife were both naked, but they felt no shame.

The serpent was the shrewdest of all the wild animals. One day he asked the woman, 'Did God really say you must not eat the fruit of any of the trees?'

The woman replied, 'It's only the fruit from the tree in the middle of the garden that we are not allowed to eat. God said, "You must not eat it; if you do, you will die."'

'You won't die!' the serpent replied. 'Your eyes will be

opened as soon as you eat it, and you will be like God, knowing both good and evil.'

The woman saw that the fruit looked delicious, and she wanted the wisdom it would give her. So she took some of the fruit and ate it. Then she gave some to her husband. At that moment their eyes were opened, and they suddenly felt shame at their nakedness. So they sewed fig leaves together to cover themselves.

Then God called to the man, 'Have you eaten from the tree whose fruit I commanded you not to eat?'

The man replied, 'It was the woman you gave me who gave me the fruit.'

Then God asked the woman, 'What have you done?'

'The serpent deceived me,' she replied.

Then God said,

> 'The ground is cursed because of you.
>> All your life you will struggle to scratch a living from it,
> You were made from dust
>> And to dust you will return.'

Then God banished them from Eden, and to the east he placed a flaming sword to guard the way to the tree of life.

Now Adam had sexual relations with his wife, Eve, and she gave birth to Cain and Abel. Abel became a shepherd, while Cain cultivated the ground.

Cain presented some of his crops to the LORD. Abel brought the best portions of the first-born lambs from his flock. The LORD accepted Abel and his gift, but he did not accept Cain and his gift. This made Cain very angry.

One day while they were in the field, Cain attacked his brother, and killed him. The LORD asked Cain, 'Where is your brother?'

'I don't know,' Cain responded. 'Am I my brother's guardian?'

The LORD said, 'Your brother's blood cries out to me from the ground! From now on you will be a homeless wanderer on the earth.'

So Cain left the LORD's presence and settled in the land of Nod, east of Eden.

ꙮꙮꙮꙮ

People began to multiply on the earth. The LORD observed the extent of human wickedness, and was sorry that he had ever made them. But Noah found favour with the LORD. So God said to Noah,

'Build a large boat! I am about to cover the earth with a flood that will destroy every living thing. So enter the boat – you and your wife and your sons and their wives. Bring a pair of every kind of animal – a male and a female – into the boat to keep them alive.'

So Noah did everything as God had commanded him.

The waters of the flood came and covered the earth, and the boat floated safely on the surface. The water covered even the highest mountains, and everything that lived on dry land died.

God remembered Noah and sent a wind to blow across the earth, and the floodwaters began to recede. Two months went by, and at last the earth was dry! Then God said,

> 'Leave the boat. Release all the animals, so they can multiply throughout the earth. I have placed my rainbow in the clouds, and when I send clouds over the earth I will remember my covenant with you and all living creatures. Never again will the flood-waters destroy all life.'

At one time all the people of the world spoke the same language, and they began saying, 'Let's build a great city with a tower that reaches to the sky.' But the LORD came down to look at the city.

'Look!' he said. 'The people are united. Come, let's go down and confuse the people with different languages.'

In that way, the LORD scattered them all over the world, and they stopped building the city.

The city was called Babel.

2

Abraham, Isaac and Jacob

This is the account of Abram, from Ur of the Chaldeans.

The Lord had said to Abram, 'Leave your native country, and go to the land that I will show you.' So Abram took his wife and all his wealth and headed for the land of Canaan.

Then God said to him,

> 'This is my covenant with you. Your name will no longer be Abram. Instead, you will be called Abraham, for you will be the father of many nations. And I will give the entire land of Canaan to you and your descendants, and I will be their God.'

One day Abraham was sitting at the entrance to his tent. He looked up and noticed three men standing nearby. When he saw them, one of them said, 'About this time next year your wife, Sarah, will have a son!'

Sarah was long past the age of having children. So she laughed silently to herself.

Then the Lord said to Abraham, 'Why did Sarah laugh? Is anything too hard for the Lord?'

The LORD kept his word and Sarah became pregnant, and gave birth to a son. Abraham named their son Isaac.

Some time later, God tested Abraham's faith. 'Abraham!' God called, 'Take your son, Isaac, and go to the land of Moriah and sacrifice him as a burnt offering on one of the mountains.'

The next morning Abraham got up early. He chopped wood for a fire for a burnt offering and placed the wood on Isaac's shoulders, while he himself carried the fire and the knife. As the two of them walked together, Isaac turned to Abraham and said, 'Father?'

'Yes, my son?' Abraham replied.

'We have the fire and the wood,' the boy said, 'but where is the sheep for the burnt offering?'

'God will provide a sheep for the burnt offering, my son,' Abraham answered.

And they both walked on together.

When they arrived at the place where God had told him to go, Abraham built an altar and arranged the wood on it. Then he tied his son, Isaac, and laid him on the altar. Abraham picked up the knife. At that moment the angel of the LORD called to him from heaven,

> 'Abraham! Don't lay a hand on the boy! For now I know that you truly fear God. You have not withheld from me even your son, your only son.'

Abraham was now a very old man, and the LORD had blessed him in every way. One day Abraham said to his oldest servant, 'Go to my homeland and find a wife there for Isaac.'

So the servant took ten of Abraham's camels with all kinds of expensive gifts, and he travelled to the town where Abraham's brother had settled. He made the camels kneel beside a well just outside the town.

It was evening, and he saw a young woman named Rebekah coming out with her water jug on her shoulder. 'Whose daughter are you?' he asked.

Now Rebekah had a brother named Laban, who ran out to meet the man at the spring. Laban said to him, 'Come and stay with us, you who are blessed by the LORD!'

So the man went home with Laban. 'I am Abraham's servant,' he explained. 'And my master made me take an oath. He said, "Go to my father's house and find a wife there for my son."'

Then Laban replied, 'The LORD has obviously brought you here. Here is Rebekah; take her and let her be the wife of your master's son.'

Then Rebekah and her servant girls mounted the camels and followed the man. When Rebekah saw Isaac, she quickly dismounted from her camel. And Isaac brought Rebekah into his tent, and she became his wife.

Abraham gave everything he owned to his son Isaac, and he breathed his last and joined his ancestors in death.

Isaac pleaded with the LORD on behalf of his wife, because she was unable to have children. The LORD answered Isaac's prayer, and Rebekah became pregnant with twins. One they named Esau; the other, Jacob.

As the boys grew up, Esau became a skilful hunter. Isaac loved Esau because he enjoyed eating the wild game Esau brought home, but Rebekah loved Jacob.

One day when Isaac was old and turning blind, he called for Esau, and said, 'Go out into the country to hunt some wild game for me. Prepare my favourite dish, and then I will pronounce the blessing that belongs to you before I die.'

But Rebekah overheard. She said to Jacob, 'Bring me two fine young goats.' So Jacob went out and got the young goats. Rebekah took them and prepared a delicious meal, just the way Isaac liked it.

Then Jacob took the food to his father. 'My father?' he said, 'It's Esau, your first-born son.'

Then Isaac said, 'Come closer, my son, bring me the wild game.' Isaac ate it, and blessed his son.

As soon as Jacob had left, Esau returned from his hunt. Esau prepared a delicious meal and brought it to his father. But Isaac asked him, 'Who are you?'

Esau replied, 'It's your son, Esau.'

Isaac began to tremble and said, 'Then who just served me wild game? I have already eaten it, and I blessed him!'

When Esau heard his father's words, he let out a bitter cry. Then Esau began to scheme: 'I will soon be mourning my father's death. Then I will kill my brother, Jacob.'

But Rebekah heard about Esau's plans. She sent for Jacob and told him.

So Jacob left. At sunset he arrived at a good place to set up camp and lay down to sleep. As he slept, he dreamed of a stairway that reached up to heaven. And he saw the angels of God going up and down the stairway. At the top stood the LORD, and he said,

'I am the God of Abraham and Isaac. The ground you are lying on belongs to you. I am giving it to you and your descendants. And all the families of the earth will be blessed through you and your descendants.'

Jacob hurried on, finally arriving in the land of the east. He saw a well in the distance. Flocks of sheep and goats lay in an open field beside it, waiting to be watered. Jacob went over to the shepherds and asked, 'Do you know a man named Laban?'

'Yes, we do,' they replied. 'Look, here comes his daughter Rachel with the flock now.'

Then Jacob explained to Rachel that he was her cousin. So Rachel quickly ran and told her father. As soon as Laban heard that Jacob had arrived, he ran out and brought him home.

After Jacob had stayed for about a month, Laban said to him, 'You shouldn't work for me without pay just because we are relatives. Tell me how much your wages should be.'

Now Laban had two daughters. The older daughter was named Leah, and the younger one was Rachel. Since Jacob was in love with Rachel, he told her father, 'I'll work for you for seven years if you'll give me Rachel as my wife.'

So Jacob worked seven years to pay for Rachel. Finally, the time came for him to marry her. So Laban invited everyone in the neighbourhood and prepared a wedding feast. But that night, when it was dark, Laban took Leah to Jacob, and he slept with her.

But when Jacob woke up in the morning – it was Leah! 'What have you done to me?' Jacob raged at Laban. 'Why have you tricked me?'

'It's not our custom here to marry off a younger daughter ahead of the first-born,' Laban replied. 'But wait until the bridal week is over; then we'll give you Rachel, too – provided you promise to work another seven years for me.'

So Jacob agreed. A week after Jacob had married Leah, Laban gave him Rachel, and he loved her. She became pregnant and gave birth to a son. She named him Joseph.

Soon after Rachel had given birth to Joseph, Jacob put his wives and children on camels and set out for the land of Canaan.

During the night a man came and wrestled with him until the dawn. When the man saw that he would not win, he said, 'Let me go, for the dawn is breaking!'

But Jacob said, 'I will not let you go unless you bless me.'

'What is your name?' the man asked.

He replied, 'Jacob.'

'Your name will no longer be Jacob,' the man told him. 'From now on you will be called Israel, because you have fought with God and with men and have won.'

3

Joseph in Egypt

Jacob settled again in the land of Canaan. Jacob loved Joseph more than any of his other children. So one day Jacob had a special gift made for Joseph – a beautiful robe. But his brothers hated Joseph, and they made plans to kill him.

But Judah said to his brothers, 'What will we gain by killing our brother?' So when traders came by, Joseph's brothers sold him to them for twenty pieces of silver. The traders took him to Egypt, where they sold Joseph to Potiphar, an officer of Pharaoh, the king of Egypt.

Joseph was a very handsome young man, and Potiphar's wife soon began to look at him lustfully. One day, she grabbed him by his cloak, demanding, 'Sleep with me!' Joseph tore himself away, but he left his cloak in her hand as he ran from the house.

She kept the cloak with her until her husband came home. Then she told him, 'That Hebrew slave you've brought into our house tried to fool around with me. But when I screamed, he ran outside, leaving his cloak with me!'

Potiphar was furious when he heard his wife's story. So he took Joseph and threw him into prison.

Some time later, Pharaoh's chief cup-bearer and chief baker offended their royal master, and he put them in the prison where Joseph was. While they were in prison, Pharaoh's cup-bearer and baker each had a dream. When Joseph saw them the next morning, the chief cup-bearer told Joseph his dream. He said,

> 'I saw a grapevine in front of me. The vine had three branches that produced clusters of ripe grapes. I was holding Pharaoh's wine cup in my hand, so I took a cluster of grapes and squeezed the juice into the cup.'

Joseph said:

> 'The three branches represent three days. Within three days Pharaoh will lift you up and restore you to your position as his chief cup-bearer. Please remember me when things go well for you. Mention me to Pharaoh, so he might let me out of this place.'

Pharaoh's birthday came three days later, and he restored the chief cup-bearer to his former position. But Pharaoh's chief cup-bearer forgot all about Joseph.

Two years later, Pharaoh was very disturbed by dreams. So he called for all the magicians and wise men of Egypt. When Pharaoh told them his dreams, not one of them could tell him what they meant. Finally, the king's chief cup-bearer spoke up. 'Some time ago there was a young Hebrew man in the prison, and he told us what our dreams meant.'

Joseph was quickly brought from the prison. Then Pharaoh said,

'I had a dream last night. In my dream I was standing on the bank of the River Nile, and I saw seven fat, healthy cows come up out of the river and begin grazing in the marsh grass. But then I saw seven sick-looking cows, scrawny and thin, come up after them. These thin cows ate the seven fat cows. But afterwards you wouldn't have known it, for they were still as thin and scrawny as before!'

Joseph responded,

'God is telling Pharaoh in advance what he is about to do. The seven healthy cows represent seven years of prosperity. The seven scrawny cows represent seven years of famine. The next seven years will be a period of great prosperity. But afterwards there will be seven years of famine.

'Therefore, Pharaoh should find a wise man and put him in charge of the entire land of Egypt. Then Pharaoh should appoint supervisors and let them gather all the food produced in the good years and bring it to Pharaoh's storehouses. That way there will be enough to eat when the seven years of famine come to the land of Egypt.'

Pharaoh asked his officials, 'Can we find anyone else like this man so obviously filled with the spirit of God?' And Pharaoh appointed him governor over all of Egypt.

Famine came, and Jacob heard that there was still grain in Egypt, so he sent his sons to buy some. The second time they went, Joseph revealed his identity to his brothers.

'I am Joseph,' he said, 'your brother, whom you sold into slavery.' Then Joseph kissed each of his brothers and wept over them.

They left Egypt and returned to their father. 'Joseph is still alive!' they told him. So Jacob and his entire family went to Egypt. Jacob lived for seventeen years in Egypt, and he breathed his last, and joined his ancestors in death.

After burying Jacob, Joseph's brothers became fearful. 'Now Joseph will show his anger and pay us back for all the wrong we did to him,' they said.

So they sent this message to Joseph: 'We, the servants of the God of your father, beg you to forgive our sin.'

But Joseph replied, 'Am I God, that I can punish you? You intended to harm me, but God intended it all for good.'

4

Moses and the exodus

In time, Joseph and all of his brothers died, ending that entire generation. But their descendants, the Israelites, multiplied so greatly that they became extremely powerful and filled the land.

Eventually, a new king came to power in Egypt who knew nothing about Joseph. He made the Israelites slaves, hoping to wear them down with crushing labour, and forcing parents to abandon their new-born babies.

At that time Moses was born. His parents cared for him at home for three months. When they had to abandon him, Pharaoh's daughter adopted him and raised him as her own son.

One day when Moses was forty years old, he decided to visit his relatives, the people of Israel. He saw an Egyptian mistreating an Israelite. So Moses came to the man's defence and avenged him, killing the Egyptian.

Pharaoh heard what had happened, and he tried to kill Moses. But Moses fled the country and lived as a foreigner in the land of Midian.

Forty years later, in the desert near Mount Sinai, an angel appeared to Moses in the flame of a burning bush.

As he went to take a closer look, the voice of God called to him from the bush,

> 'I am the God of Abraham, Isaac and Jacob. I have seen the oppression of my people in Egypt. So I have come down to rescue them. Now go, for I am sending you to Pharaoh. You must lead my people out of Egypt.'

But Moses protested, 'If I go to the people of Israel and tell them, "The God of your ancestors has sent me to you," they will ask me, "What is his name?" Then what should I tell them?' God replied to Moses, 'I AM WHO I AM. This is my eternal name.'

But Moses pleaded with the LORD, 'O Lord, I'm not very good with words. Lord, please! Send anyone else.'

Then the LORD became angry with Moses. 'All right,' he said. 'What about your brother, Aaron? I know he speaks well. I will instruct you both in what to do.'

After this, Moses and Aaron went and spoke to Pharaoh. They told him, 'The LORD, the God of Israel, says: Let my people go.'

'Is that so?' retorted Pharaoh. 'And who is the LORD? Why should I listen to him?'

Then the LORD told Moses, 'Now you will see what I will do to Pharaoh. Announce to him, "The LORD will strike the water of the Nile."' So Moses and Aaron did as the LORD commanded. Suddenly, the whole river turned to blood! But Pharaoh returned to his palace.

Then the LORD said to Moses, 'Go back to Pharaoh and

announce to him, "Let my people go. If you refuse, I will send a plague of frogs; dust will turn into swarms of gnats; and I will send swarms of flies."'

But Pharaoh refused to let the people go.

'Go back to Pharaoh,' the LORD commanded Moses. 'Tell him, "The hand of the LORD will strike all your livestock with a deadly plague."'

But Pharaoh still refused to let the people go.

Then the LORD said, 'Take handfuls of soot from a brick kiln, and toss it into the air.'

As Pharaoh watched, Moses threw the soot into the air, and boils broke out on people and animals alike.

Then the LORD sent thunder and hail, and lightning flashed towards the earth. And the LORD brought locusts over the whole land. They devoured every plant.

Then Moses lifted his hand to the sky, and a deep darkness covered the entire land of Egypt for three days.

But Pharaoh would not let them go.

Then the LORD said to Moses, 'I will strike Pharaoh with one more blow. After that, Pharaoh will let you leave. Tell all the Israelite men and women:

"Each family must choose a lamb or a young goat for a sacrifice. They are to take some of the blood and smear it on the sides and top of the door-frames of the houses where they eat the animal. This is the LORD's Passover. On that night I will pass through the land of Egypt and strike down every first-born son in the land of Egypt.

"I will execute judgement against all the gods of Egypt, for I am the LORD! But the blood on your doorposts will serve as a sign. When I see the blood, I will pass over you. This is a day to remember. Each year, from generation to generation, you must celebrate it as a special festival to the LORD.'"

The people of Israel did just as the LORD had commanded. That night, the LORD struck down all the first-born sons in the land of Egypt, and loud wailing was heard throughout the land.

Pharaoh sent for Moses and Aaron. 'Get out!' he ordered. 'Leave my people – and take the rest of the Israelites with you!'

That night the people of Israel left. There were about 600,000 men, plus all the women and children.

The people of Israel had lived in Egypt for 430 years.

5

Israel in the wilderness

When Pharaoh finally let the people go, God led them through the wilderness towards the Red Sea. Then the LORD gave these instructions to Moses: 'Order the Israelites to camp there along the shore.'

When the Israelites had fled, Pharaoh and his officials changed their minds. Pharaoh called up his troops. He took with him Egypt's best chariots, each with its commander. He chased after the people of Israel, and as Pharaoh approached, the LORD said to Moses, 'Divide the water so the Israelites can walk through the middle of the sea on dry ground.'

Then Moses raised his hand over the sea, and the people of Israel walked through the middle, with walls of water on each side!

The Egyptians chased them. But when all the Israelites had reached the other side, Moses raised his hand over the sea, and the water rushed back and covered the entire army of Pharaoh. Not a single one survived.

Two months after the Israelites left Egypt, they arrived at Mount Sinai. Then Moses climbed the mountain to appear before God. The LORD called to him from the mountain,

'Give these instructions to the descendants of Israel: "You have seen what I did to the Egyptians. You know how I carried you on eagles' wings and brought you to myself. Now if you will obey me and keep my covenant, you will be my holy nation."'

Then the LORD told Moses, 'Go down and prepare the people for my arrival. Consecrate them today and tomorrow, and be sure they are ready on the third day.'

On the third day, thunder roared and lightning flashed. A dense cloud came down on the mountain, and all the people trembled. Moses led them out from the camp to meet with God, and they stood at the foot of the mountain. All of Mount Sinai was covered with smoke because the LORD had descended on it in the form of fire. The smoke billowed into the sky, and the whole mountain shook violently.

Then God gave these instructions:

'I am the LORD your God, who rescued you from the land of Egypt.
You must not have any other god but me.
You must not make for yourself an idol of any kind.
You must not misuse the name of the LORD your God.
Remember to observe the Sabbath day by keeping it holy.
Honour your father and mother.
You must not murder.
You must not commit adultery.
You must not steal.
You must not testify falsely against your neighbour.

You must not covet anything that belongs to your neighbour.'

Early the next morning Moses built an altar at the foot of the mountain. He also set up twelve pillars, one for each of the twelve tribes of Israel.

Then the LORD said to Moses, 'I will give you tablets of stone on which I have inscribed the commands so you can teach the people.' So Moses and his assistant Joshua set out, and climbed up the mountain. Moses remained on the mountain forty days and forty nights.

When the people saw how long it was taking Moses to come back, they gathered around Aaron. 'Come on,' they said, 'make us some gods who can lead us. We don't know what happened to this fellow Moses.'

So all the people took the gold rings from their ears and brought them to Aaron. Then Aaron took the gold, melted it down, and moulded it into the shape of a calf. When the people saw it, they exclaimed, 'O Israel, these are the gods who brought you out of the land of Egypt!'

Then Moses went down the mountain. He held in his hands the stone tablets inscribed with the terms of the covenant. When Joshua heard the people shouting, he exclaimed to Moses, 'It sounds like war in the camp!'

When they came near, Moses saw the calf and the dancing, and he burned with anger. He threw the stone tablets to the ground. He took the calf they had made and burned it. Then he ground it into powder, threw it into the water, and forced the people to drink it.

Then the LORD sent a great plague upon the people because they had worshipped the calf Aaron had made.

Forty years after the Israelites left Egypt, Moses addressed the people.

'Listen, O Israel! The LORD is our God, the LORD alone. You must love the LORD your God with all your heart, all your soul, and all your strength. And you must commit yourselves wholeheartedly to these commands that I am giving you today. Repeat them again and again to your children.

'Appoint judges for yourselves from each of your tribes in all the towns the LORD your God is giving you. They must judge the people fairly. Let true justice prevail, so you may occupy the land that the LORD your God is giving you.'

Then Moses went up to Mount Nebo from the plains of Moab. And the LORD showed him the whole land; all the land of Ephraim; all the land of Judah, extending to the Mediterranean Sea.

Then the LORD said to Moses, 'This is the land I promised on oath to Abraham, Isaac, and Jacob. I have now allowed you to see it, but you will not enter the land.'

So Moses, the servant of the LORD, died. There has never been another prophet in Israel like Moses, whom the LORD knew face to face.

6

The Promised Land

After the death of Moses, the LORD spoke to Joshua. He said, 'The time has come for you to lead the Israelites into the land I am giving them.'

Then Joshua secretly sent out two spies from the Israelite camp. He instructed them, 'Scout out the land on the other side of the River Jordan, especially around Jericho.'

So the two men set out and came to the house of a prostitute named Rahab and stayed there that night. But someone told the king of Jericho, so the king sent orders to Rahab: 'Bring out the men who have come into your house.'

Rahab had taken them up to the roof and hidden them beneath bundles of flax. Then, since Rahab's house was built into the town wall, she let them down by a rope through the window. The two spies crossed the River Jordan, and reported to Joshua all that had happened.

Now the gates of Jericho were tightly shut because the people were afraid of the Israelites. So Joshua called together the priests and said, 'Assign seven priests to walk in front, each carrying a ram's horn.' Then he gave orders to the people: 'March around the town, and the armed men will lead the way.'

They followed this pattern for six days. On the seventh day, Joshua commanded the people, 'Shout! For the LORD has given you the town!'

When the people shouted, the walls of Jericho collapsed, and the Israelites charged into the town and captured it. They completely destroyed everything in it – men and women, young and old.

Meanwhile, the spies went in and brought out Rahab and all the relatives who were with her. So Joshua spared Rahab, because she had hidden the spies.

Joshua took control of the entire land. He gave it to the people of Israel, dividing the land among the tribes.

⧖ ⧖ ⧖ ⧖

The years passed, and Joshua, who was now very old, called together all the elders of Israel. He said to them,

'Be very careful to follow everything Moses wrote in the Book of Instruction. If you break the covenant of the LORD by worshipping other gods, you will quickly vanish from the good land he has given you.'

The people said to Joshua, 'We will serve the LORD our God. We will obey him alone.'

After this, Joshua died, and another generation grew up who did evil in the LORD's sight and served the images of Baal. They abandoned the LORD, the God of their ancestors, who had brought them out of Egypt. This made the LORD burn with anger against Israel, so he turned them over to their enemies all around.

Then the LORD raised up judges to rescue the Israelites. Whenever the LORD raised up a judge, he was with that judge and rescued the people from their enemies. But when the judge died, the people returned to their corrupt ways, behaving worse than those who had lived before them.

7

Samson and Delilah

The Israelites did evil, and served the images of Baal. Then the LORD burned with anger against Israel. But when Israel cried out for help, the LORD raised up a rescuer to save them. His name was Samson. Samson judged Israel for twenty years during the period when the Philistines dominated the land.

One day Samson went to the Philistine town of Gaza and spent the night with a prostitute. Word soon spread that Samson was there, so the men of Gaza gathered and waited all night at the town gates, saying to themselves, 'When morning comes, we will kill him.'

But Samson stayed in bed only until midnight. Then he got up, took hold of the doors of the town gate, including the two posts, and lifted them up, bar and all. He put them on his shoulders and carried them all the way to the top of the hill across from Hebron.

Some time later, Samson fell in love with a woman named Delilah. The rulers of the Philistines went to her and said, 'Entice Samson to tell you what makes him so strong and how he can be overpowered and tied up securely. Then each of us will give you 1,100 pieces of silver.'

So Delilah said to Samson, 'Please tell me what makes you so strong and what it would take to tie you up securely.'

Samson replied, 'If I were tied up with seven new bowstrings that have not yet been dried, I would become as weak as anyone else.'

So the Philistine rulers brought Delilah seven new bowstrings, and she tied Samson up with them. She had hidden some men in one of the inner rooms of her house, and she cried out, 'Samson! The Philistines have come to capture you!' But Samson snapped the bowstrings as a piece of string snaps when it is burned by a fire.

Then Delilah pouted, 'How can you tell me, "I love you," when you don't share your secrets with me?' She tormented him with her nagging day after day.

Finally, Samson shared his secret with her. 'My hair has never been cut,' he confessed, 'for I was dedicated to God from birth. If my head were shaved, my strength would leave me.'

Delilah realized he had told her the truth, so she sent for the Philistine rulers. Delilah lulled Samson to sleep with his head in her lap, and then she called in a man to shave off the seven locks of his hair. Then she cried out, 'Samson! The Philistines have come to capture you!'

When he woke up, he thought, 'I will do as before and shake myself free.' But he didn't realize the Lord had left him. So the Philistines captured him and gouged out his eyes. They took him to Gaza, where he was bound with bronze chains and forced to grind grain in the prison.

But before long, his hair began to grow back.

The Philistine rulers held a great festival, offering sacrifices and praising their god, Dagon. They said, 'Our god has given us victory over our enemy Samson!'

Half drunk by now, the people demanded, 'Bring out Samson so he can amuse us!' So he was brought from the prison, and they had him stand between the pillars supporting the roof.

Samson said to the young servant who was leading him by the hand, 'Place my hands against the pillars that hold up the temple. I want to rest against them.' Now the temple was completely filled with people. All the Philistine rulers were there.

Samson prayed, 'O God, please strengthen me just one more time.' Then Samson put his hands on the pillars. Pushing against them, he prayed, 'Let me die with the Philistines.' And the temple crashed down on all the people.

He killed more when he died than he had during his entire lifetime.

8

The story of Ruth

In the days when the judges ruled in Israel, a severe famine came upon the land. So a man from Bethlehem in Judah went to live in the country of Moab, taking his wife and two sons with him. The man's name was Elimelech, and his wife was Naomi. Their two sons were Mahlon and Kilion.

Then Elimelech died, and Naomi was left with her two sons. The two sons married Moabite women. One married a woman named Orpah, and the other a woman named Ruth. But about ten years later, both Mahlon and Kilion died.

Then Naomi heard that the LORD had blessed his people in Judah by giving them good crops again. So Naomi and her daughters-in-law got ready to return to her homeland.

But Naomi said to her two daughters-in-law, 'Go back to your mothers' homes. And may the LORD bless you.' Then they all broke down and wept, and Orpah kissed her mother-in-law goodbye.

But Ruth replied, 'Wherever you go, I will go. Your people will be my people, and your God will be my God!'

So the two of them continued on their journey. They arrived in Bethlehem at the beginning of the barley harvest. Now there was a wealthy and influential man in Bethlehem named Boaz, who was a relative of Naomi's husband.

One day Ruth went out to gather grain behind the harvesters. And as it happened, she found herself working in a field that belonged to Boaz. While she was there, Boaz went over and said to Ruth, 'Listen, my daughter. Stay right here with us when you gather grain. I have warned the young men not to treat you roughly.'

So Ruth gathered barley there all day, and when she beat out the grain that evening, it filled an entire basket. She carried it back into town and told her mother-in-law about the man in whose field she had worked.

Naomi said to Ruth,

'My daughter, Boaz is a close relative of ours. Tonight he will be winnowing barley at the threshing floor. Now do as I tell you – take a bath and put on perfume and dress in your nicest clothes. Then go to the threshing floor, but don't let Boaz see you until he has finished eating and drinking. Be sure to notice where he lies down; then go and uncover his feet and lie down there.'

So she went down to the threshing floor that night and followed the instructions of her mother-in-law.

After Boaz had finished eating and drinking and was in good spirits, he lay down at the far end of the pile of grain and went to sleep. Then Ruth came quietly, uncovered his feet, and lay down. Around midnight Boaz suddenly woke up and turned over. He was surprised to find a woman lying at his feet!

'Who are you?' he asked.

'I am your servant Ruth,' she replied. 'Spread the corner of your covering over me, for you are my family redeemer.' So Ruth lay at Boaz's feet until the morning, but she got up before it was light.

When Ruth told Naomi everything Boaz had done for her, Naomi said, 'Just be patient, my daughter, until we hear what happens.'

Boaz went to the town gate and took a seat there. Then he said to the elders and to the crowd standing around, 'Today I have bought from Naomi all the property of Elimelech. And with the land I have acquired Ruth, the Moabite widow, to be my wife.'

So Boaz took Ruth into his home, and she became his wife. The LORD enabled her to become pregnant, and she gave birth to a son. She named him Obed. He became the father of Jesse and Jesse was the father of David.

9

Samuel, Saul and David

There was a man named Elkanah who had two wives, Hannah and Peninnah. Peninnah had children, but Hannah did not. Hannah was in deep anguish, and she made this vow: 'O Lord, if you will answer my prayer and give me a son, then I will give him back to you for his entire lifetime.'

The Lord remembered her plea, and in due time she gave birth to a son. She named him Samuel. When the child was weaned, the boy served the Lord by assisting Eli the priest.

As Samuel grew up, the Lord was with him, and all Israel knew Samuel as a prophet of the Lord.

As Samuel grew old, the elders of Israel told him, 'Give us a king to judge us like all the other nations have.'

Samuel was displeased and went to the Lord for guidance. 'Do everything they say to you,' the Lord replied, 'for they are rejecting me, not you.'

Later, Samuel brought all the tribes of Israel before the Lord, and Saul was chosen from among them. But when they looked for him, he had disappeared! So they asked the Lord, 'Where is he?'

The LORD replied, 'He is hiding among the baggage.' So they found him and brought him out.

And all the people shouted, 'Long live the king!'

Now the Israelites fought constantly with the Philistines throughout Saul's lifetime. The Philistines mustered their army for battle and camped in Judah. Saul countered by gathering his troops near the valley of Elah. So the Philistines and Israelites faced each other on opposite hills, with the valley between them.

Then Goliath, a Philistine champion from Gath, came out of the Philistine ranks. He was over three metres tall! He stood and shouted a taunt across to the Israelites.

'Choose one man to come down here and fight me! If he kills me, then we will be your slaves. But if I kill him, you will be our slaves!'

When Saul and the Israelites heard this, they were deeply shaken.

Now David was the son of a man named Jesse, from Bethlehem in Judah. Jesse had eight sons. Jesse's three oldest sons had already joined Saul's army. David was the youngest son. David's three oldest brothers stayed with Saul's army, but David went back and forth so he could help his father with the sheep in Bethlehem.

One day Jesse said to David, 'Take these loaves of bread, and carry them quickly to your brothers.' So David hurried out to greet his brothers. As he was talking with them, Goliath came out from the Philistine ranks.

As soon as the Israelite army saw him, they began to run away in fright. 'Have you seen the giant?' the men asked. 'He comes out each day to defy Israel. The king has offered a huge reward to anyone who kills him.'

David asked the soldiers, 'Who is this pagan Philistine, that he is allowed to defy the armies of the living God?' And he picked up five smooth stones from a stream and put them into his shepherd's bag. Then, armed only with his staff and sling, he started across the valley to fight the Philistine.

Goliath walked out towards David, sneering in contempt at this ruddy-faced boy. 'Am I a dog,' he roared at David, 'that you come at me with a stick? Come over here, and I'll give your flesh to the birds!'

David replied to the Philistine, 'You come to me with sword, spear, and javelin, but I come to you in the name of the God of the armies of Israel.'

As Goliath moved closer to attack, David quickly ran out to meet him. Reaching into his shepherd's bag and taking out a stone, he hurled it with his sling and hit the Philistine in the forehead. The stone sank in, and Goliath stumbled and fell face down on the ground. Then David ran over and pulled Goliath's sword from its sheath and cut off his head.

When the Philistines saw that their champion was dead, they turned and ran. Then David took the Philistine's head to Jerusalem.

As Saul watched David go out to fight the Philistine, he asked Abner, the commander of his army, 'Abner, whose son is this young man?'

'I really don't know,' Abner declared.

'Well, find out who he is!' the king told him.

As soon as David returned from killing Goliath, Abner brought him to Saul with the Philistine's head still in his hand.

After David had finished talking with Saul, he met Jonathan, the king's son. There was an immediate bond between them, and Jonathan made a solemn pact with David, because he loved him as he loved himself.

Whatever Saul asked David to do, David did it successfully. So Saul made him a commander over the men of war. When the victorious Israelite army was returning home, women from all the towns of Israel sang and danced for joy with tambourines and cymbals. This was their song:

> 'Saul has killed his thousands,
> and David his ten thousands!'

From that time on Saul kept a jealous eye on David.

Later, the Philistines mustered their armies for another war with Israel, and the men of Israel fled before them. The Philistines closed in on Saul. They killed his sons and wounded him severely.

Saul groaned to his armour bearer, 'Take your sword and kill me before these pagan Philistines come to run me through and taunt and torture me.' But his armour bearer was afraid and would not do it. So Saul took his own sword and fell on it.

David composed a funeral song:

> 'Oh, how the mighty heroes have fallen!
>> How beloved and gracious were Saul and
>>> Jonathan!
> How I weep for you, my brother Jonathan!
>> Your love for me was deep,
>> deeper than the love of women!'

After this, David made a covenant before the LORD with all the elders of Israel. And they anointed him king of Israel.

♙♙♙♙

When David was settled in his palace, the king summoned Nathan the prophet. But that same night the LORD said to Nathan,

> 'Go and tell my servant David, "This is what the LORD has declared: I took you from tending sheep and selected you to be the leader of my people. When you are buried with your ancestors, I will raise up one of your descendants and I will make his kingdom strong. He will build a house – a temple – for my name. And I will secure his royal throne for ever."'

So Nathan went to David and told him everything the LORD had said.

Then King David went in and sat before the Lord and prayed,

> 'How great you are, O Sovereign Lord! There is no one like you. What other nation have you redeemed from slavery to be your own people? May your name be honoured for ever.'

After this, David subdued the Philistines, and the Lord made David victorious wherever he went. Joab was commander of the army. In the spring of the year, when kings go out to war, David sent Joab and the Israelite army to fight the Ammonites. However, David stayed behind in Jerusalem.

Late one afternoon, after his midday rest, David got out of bed and was walking on the roof of the palace. As he looked out over the city, he noticed a woman of unusual beauty taking a bath. He sent someone to find out who she was, and he was told, 'She is Bathsheba, the wife of Uriah the Hittite.' Then David sent messengers to get her; and when she came to the palace, he slept with her. Then she returned home. Later, Bathsheba sent David a message, saying, 'I'm pregnant.'

Then David sent word to Joab: 'Send me Uriah the Hittite.' When Uriah arrived, David asked him how the war was progressing. Then he told Uriah, 'Go on home and relax.' But Uriah didn't go home. He slept that night at the palace entrance with the king's palace guard.

Then David invited him to dinner and got him drunk. But even then he couldn't get Uriah to go home to his wife.

So the next morning David wrote a letter to Joab and gave it to Uriah to deliver. The letter instructed Joab, 'Station Uriah on the front lines where the battle is fiercest. Then pull back so that he will be killed.'

So Joab assigned Uriah to a spot close to the city wall where he knew the enemy's strongest men were fighting. And when the enemy soldiers came out of the city to fight, Uriah the Hittite was killed.

When Uriah's wife heard that her husband was dead, she mourned for him. When the period of mourning was over, David sent for her and brought her to the palace, and she became one of his wives.

But the LORD was displeased with what David had done.

Now David's son Absalom was praised as the most handsome man in all Israel. He was flawless from head to foot. He lived in Jerusalem for two years, but he never got to see the king. Then Absalom bought a chariot and horses, and he hired fifty bodyguards to run ahead of him. He said to the king, 'Let me go to Hebron to offer a sacrifice to the LORD and fulfil a vow I made to him.'

So Absalom went to Hebron. But while he was there, he sent secret messengers to all the tribes of Israel to stir up a rebellion against the king. 'As soon as you hear the ram's horn,' his message read, 'you are to say, "Absalom has been crowned king in Hebron."' He took men from Jerusalem with him as guests. Soon many others also joined Absalom, and the conspiracy gained momentum.

A messenger soon arrived in Jerusalem to tell David, 'All Israel has joined Absalom in a conspiracy against you!'

So the king mustered the men who were with him and gave this command to Joab: 'For my sake, deal gently with young Absalom.'

The battle began in the forest of Ephraim, and the Israelite troops were beaten back by David's men. During the battle, Absalom happened to come upon some of David's men. He tried to escape on his mule, but as he rode beneath the thick branches of a great tree, his hair got caught in the tree. His mule kept going and left him dangling in the air.

One of David's men saw what had happened and told Joab. He took three daggers and plunged them into Absalom's heart as he dangled, still alive, in the great tree.

Then Joab said to a man from Ethiopia, 'Go and tell the king what you have seen.' The man bowed and ran off.

While David was sitting between the gates of the town, the man from Ethiopia arrived and said, 'I have good news for my lord the king. Today the LORD has rescued you from all those who rebelled against you.'

'What about young Absalom?' the king demanded. 'Is he all right?'

And the Ethiopian replied, 'May all of your enemies, my lord the king, share the fate of that young man!'

The king was overcome. He went up to the room over the gateway and as he went, he cried, 'O my son Absalom! My son, my son Absalom! If only I had died instead of you! O Absalom, my son, my son.'

10

Solomon the sage

As the time of King David's death approached, he gave this charge to his son Solomon:

> 'I am going where everyone on earth must go. Take courage and be a man. Keep the commands written in the Law of Moses. If you do this, then the LORD will keep the promise he made to me. He told me, "If your descendants follow me faithfully, one of them will always sit on the throne of Israel."'

Then David died and Solomon became king.

The LORD appeared to Solomon in a dream, and said, 'Ask, and I will give it to you!' Solomon replied, 'Give me an understanding heart so that I can govern your people well.'

The LORD was pleased that Solomon had asked for wisdom.

Some time later, two prostitutes came to the king to have an argument settled. 'Please, my lord,' one of them began,

'This woman and I live in the same house. I gave birth to a baby while she was with me in the house. Three days later, this woman also had a baby. But her baby died during the night when she rolled over on it. Then she got up and took my son from beside me while I was asleep. She laid her dead child in my arms and took mine to sleep beside her. And in the morning when I tried to nurse my son, he was dead! But when I looked more closely in the morning light, I saw that it wasn't my son at all.'

Then the other woman interrupted, 'It certainly was your son, and the living child is mine.'

The king said, 'Bring me a sword.' Then he said, 'Cut the living child in two, and give half to one woman and half to the other!'

Then the woman who was the real mother of the living child cried out, 'Oh no, my lord! Give her the child – please do not kill him!'

But the other woman said, 'All right, he will be neither yours nor mine; divide him between us!'

Then the king said, 'Do not kill the child, but give him to the woman who wants him to live, for she is his mother!'

When all Israel heard the king's decision, the people were in awe of the king, for they saw the wisdom God had given him for rendering justice.

During the fourth year of Solomon's reign, he began to construct the Temple of the LORD. This was 480 years after the people of Israel were rescued from their slavery in Egypt.

It took seven years to build the Temple.

When the queen of Sheba heard of Solomon's fame, she came to Jerusalem with a large group of attendants and a great caravan of camels laden with spices, large quantities of gold and precious jewels. When she met with Solomon, she exclaimed, 'Your wisdom and prosperity are far beyond what I was told. How happy your people must be!'

So King Solomon became richer and wiser than any other king on earth. People from every nation came to consult him and to hear the wisdom God had given him.

Now King Solomon loved many foreign women. And in Solomon's old age, they turned his heart to worship other gods. The LORD was very angry with Solomon. So the LORD raised up a rebel leader, Jeroboam, one of Solomon's own officials. Solomon tried to kill Jeroboam, but he fled to Egypt and stayed there until Solomon died.

Solomon ruled in Jerusalem for forty years. When he died, his son Rehoboam became the next king. When Jeroboam heard of this, he returned from Egypt. The leaders of Israel summoned him and went to speak with Rehoboam. 'Your father was a hard master,' they said. 'Lighten the harsh labour demands and heavy taxes that your father imposed on us. Then we will be your loyal subjects.'

Rehoboam replied, 'My father beat you with whips, but I will beat you with scorpions!'

When all Israel realized that the king had refused to listen to them, they responded,

'Down with the dynasty of David!'

So the people of Israel returned home. But Rehoboam continued to rule over the towns of Judah.

When the people learned of Jeroboam's return from Egypt, they called an assembly and made him king over Israel. Jeroboam then built up the city of Shechem in the hill country of Ephraim, and it became his capital.

Later, he made two gold calves. He said to the people, 'Look, Israel, these are the gods who brought you out of Egypt!'

11
Elijah the prophet

When Rehoboam died, his son Abijam became king over Judah. When Abijam died, his son Asa became king, and there was constant war between Judah and Israel.

When Jeroboam died, his son Nadab became king over Israel. Then Baasha assassinated him, and he became the next king of Israel. He immediately slaughtered all the descendants of Jeroboam, so that not one of the royal family was left.

When Baasha died, his son Elah became king. Then Zimri, who commanded the royal chariots, struck him down and became king. But Omri, commander of the army, led the entire army of Israel to attack Zimri, and Omri became the next king.

When Omri died, his son Ahab reigned in Samaria. He did what was evil in the LORD's sight, even more than any of the kings before him. He married Jezebel, the daughter of King Ethbaal of the Sidonians, and he built a temple for Baal in Samaria.

It was during his reign that Elijah told King Ahab, 'Summon all Israel to join me at Mount Carmel, along with the prophets of Baal who are supported by Jezebel.' So

Ahab summoned all the people of Israel and the prophets to Mount Carmel.

Then Elijah stood in front of them and said, 'How much longer will you waver, hobbling between two opinions? If the LORD is God, follow him! But if Baal is God, then follow him!' But the people were completely silent.

Then Elijah said to them,

'I am the only prophet of the LORD who is left, but Baal has 450 prophets. Now bring two bulls. The prophets of Baal may choose whichever one they wish and cut it into pieces and lay it on the wood of their altar, but without setting fire to it. I will prepare the other bull. Then call on the name of your god, and I will call on the name of the LORD. The god who answers by setting fire to the wood is the true God!'

And all the people agreed.

The prophets of Baal prepared one of the bulls and placed it on the altar. Then they called on the name of Baal from morning until noontime, shouting, 'O Baal, answer us!' But there was no reply.

About midday Elijah began mocking them. 'You'll have to shout louder,' he scoffed, 'for surely he is a god! Perhaps he is daydreaming, or is relieving himself. Or maybe he is asleep and needs to be wakened!'

So they shouted louder, and they cut themselves with knives and swords until the blood gushed out. They raved all afternoon until the time of the evening sacrifice, but still there was no response.

Then Elijah called to the people, 'Come over here!' They all crowded around him as he repaired the altar of the LORD that had been torn down. Then he dug a trench around the altar. He piled wood on the altar, cut the bull into pieces, and laid the pieces on the wood.

Then he said, 'Fill four large jars with water, and pour the water over the offering and the wood.' So they did as he said, and the water ran around the altar and even filled the trench.

Elijah the prophet walked up to the altar and prayed, 'O LORD, God of Abraham, Isaac, and Jacob, prove today that you are God in Israel and that I am your servant.'

Immediately the fire of the LORD flashed down from heaven and burned up the young bull, the wood, the stones, and the dust. It even licked up all the water in the trench! And when all the people saw it, they fell face down on the ground and cried out, 'The LORD – he is God!'

Then Elijah commanded, 'Seize all the prophets of Baal. Don't let a single one escape!' So the people seized them all, and Elijah took them down to the Kishon Valley and killed them there.

Ahab told Jezebel everything Elijah had done, including the way he had killed all the prophets of Baal. So Jezebel sent this message to Elijah: 'May the gods strike me if by this time tomorrow I have not killed you just as you killed them.'

Elijah was afraid and fled to a town in Judah. Then he

went on alone into the wilderness, travelling all day. He sat down under a solitary broom tree and prayed that he might die.

But as he was sleeping, an angel touched him and told him, 'Get up and eat!' He looked around and there beside his head was some bread and a jar of water! So he got up and ate and drank, and the food gave him enough strength to travel forty days and forty nights to Mount Sinai, the mountain of God. There he came to a cave, where he spent the night.

The LORD said to him, 'Go out and stand before me on the mountain.' And as Elijah stood there, the LORD passed by, and a mighty windstorm hit the mountain, but the LORD was not in the wind. After the wind there was an earthquake, but the LORD was not in the earthquake. And after the earthquake there was a fire, but the LORD was not in the fire.

And after the fire there was the sound of a gentle whisper.

When Elijah heard it, he wrapped his face in his cloak and went out and stood at the entrance of the cave. And a voice said, 'What are you doing here, Elijah?'

He replied,

'I have zealously served God Almighty. But the people of Israel have broken their covenant with you, torn down your altars, and killed every one of your prophets. I am the only one left, and now they are trying to kill me, too.'

Then the LORD told him, 'Go back the same way you came, and anoint Elisha to replace you as my prophet.'

Elijah found Elisha ploughing a field. Elijah went over to him and threw his cloak across his shoulders and then walked away. So Elisha went with Elijah as his assistant.

After King Ahab's death, Elijah and Elisha were travelling beside the River Jordan. As they were walking along, suddenly a chariot of fire appeared, drawn by horses of fire. It drove between the two men, separating them, and Elijah was carried by a whirlwind into heaven.

12

The story of Jonah

The Lord gave this message to Jonah: 'Go to the great city of Nineveh. Announce my judgement against it because I have seen how wicked its people are.' But Jonah went in the opposite direction to get away from the Lord. He went down to the port of Joppa, where he found a ship leaving for Tarshish. He bought a ticket and went on board.

But the Lord hurled a powerful wind over the sea, causing a violent storm that threatened to break the ship apart. Fearing for their lives, the desperate sailors shouted to their gods for help and cast lots to see which of them had offended the gods and caused the terrible storm. When they did this, the lots identified Jonah as the culprit.

'Throw me into the sea,' Jonah said, 'and it will become calm again. I know that this terrible storm is all my fault.'

Then the sailors picked Jonah up and threw him into the raging sea, and the storm stopped at once!

Now the Lord had arranged for a great fish to swallow Jonah. And Jonah was inside the fish for three days and three nights.

The Lord ordered the fish to spit Jonah out on to the beach. Then the Lord spoke to Jonah a second time: 'Go to the great city of Nineveh, and deliver the message I have given you.'

This time Jonah obeyed and the people of Nineveh believed God's message. They declared a fast and put on sackcloth to show their sorrow. When God saw, he changed his mind and did not carry out the destruction he had threatened.

This change of plans greatly upset Jonah, and he complained to the LORD about it. Then Jonah went out to the east side of the city and made a shelter to sit under as he waited to see what would happen.

God arranged for a leafy plant to grow there, and soon it spread its broad leaves over Jonah's head, shading him from the sun. This eased his discomfort, and Jonah was very grateful for the plant.

But God also arranged for a worm! The next morning at dawn the worm ate through the plant so that it withered away. And as the sun grew hot, God arranged for a scorching east wind to blow on Jonah until he grew faint and wished to die.

Then God said to Jonah, 'Is it right for you to be angry because the plant died?'

'Yes,' Jonah retorted, 'angry enough to die!'

Then the LORD said, 'You feel sorry about the plant, though you did nothing to put it there. It came quickly and died quickly. But Nineveh has more than 120,000 people living in spiritual darkness, not to mention all the animals. Shouldn't I feel sorry for such a great city?'

13

Exile and return

Some time later, the king of Assyria invaded the land, and for three years he besieged the city of Samaria. Finally Samaria fell, and the people of Israel were exiled to Assyria.

This disaster came upon the people of Israel because they sinned against the LORD, who had rescued them from Egypt. They rejected the LORD and worshipped Baal and all the forces of heaven. They even sacrificed their own sons and daughters in the fire.

Because the LORD was very angry, he swept them away from his presence. Only the tribe of Judah remained in the land. But even the people of Judah refused to obey the commands of God, desecrating the Temple of the LORD in Jerusalem. The LORD repeatedly sent his prophets to warn them. But the people despised their words.

So the LORD brought the king of Babylon against them. The Babylonians had no pity on the people, killing both young men and young women, the old and the infirm. God handed all of them over to Nebuchadnezzar.

The king took all the treasures from the LORD's Temple. Then his army burned the Temple, tore down the walls of

Jerusalem, burned all the palaces, and destroyed everything of value.

The few who survived were taken as exiles to Babylon, and they became servants to the king until the kingdom of Persia came to power.

🕱🕱🕱🕱

King Nebuchadnezzar ordered his chief of staff to bring to the palace some of the young men of Judah's royal family, who had been brought to Babylon as captives. God gave these young men wisdom. And God gave Daniel the special ability to interpret visions and dreams.

Many years later, King Belshazzar gave a great feast, and he gave orders to bring in the gold and silver cups that Nebuchadnezzar had taken from the Temple in Jerusalem. The king and his nobles, his wives, and his concubines drank from them.

Suddenly, they saw the fingers of a human hand writing on the wall of the king's palace. The king himself saw the hand, and his face turned pale with fright. The king shouted for the astrologers and fortune-tellers. But none of them could tell him what it meant.

So Daniel was brought in before the king. The king asked him, 'Are you Daniel, from Judah? I have heard that you have the spirit of the gods within you. If you can read these words and tell me their meaning, you will become the third highest ruler in the kingdom.'

Daniel answered the king, 'This is the message that

was written: MENE, MENE, TEKEL, and PARSIN. *Mene* means "numbered" – God has numbered the days of your reign and has brought it to an end. *Tekel* means "weighed" – you have been weighed on the balances and have not measured up. *Parsin* means "divided" – your kingdom has been divided and given to the Medes and Persians.'

Then at Belshazzar's command, Daniel was proclaimed the third highest ruler in the kingdom.

That very night Belshazzar, the Babylonian king, was killed. And Darius the Mede took over the kingdom.

Darius chose Daniel and two others as administrators to protect the king's interests. Because of Daniel's great ability, the king made plans to place him over the entire empire. Then the other high officers began searching for some fault in the way Daniel was handling government affairs, but they couldn't find anything. So they concluded, 'Our only chance of finding grounds for accusing Daniel will be in connection with his religion.'

So the officers went to the king and said,

'Long live King Darius! We are all in agreement that the king should make a law that will be strictly enforced. Give orders that for the next thirty days any person who prays to anyone, divine or human – except to you, Your Majesty – will be thrown into the den of lions. And now, Your Majesty, issue and sign this law so it cannot be revoked.'

So King Darius signed the law.

But when Daniel learned that the law had been signed, he went home and prayed three times a day, just as he had always done. Then the officials told the king, 'That man Daniel is ignoring you and your law.'

So the king gave orders for Daniel to be arrested and thrown into the den of lions. A stone was brought and placed over the mouth of the den.

Early the next morning, the king got up and hurried out to the lions' den. When he got there, he called out in anguish, 'Daniel, was your God able to rescue you?'

Daniel answered, 'Long live the king! My God sent his angel to shut the lions' mouths, for I have been found innocent in his sight.'

The king was overjoyed and ordered that Daniel be lifted from the den. Then Darius sent this message to the people of every nation throughout the world:

'I decree that everyone throughout my kingdom should tremble with fear before the God of Daniel. For he is the living God. His kingdom will never be destroyed, and his rule will never end.'

⧖ ⧖ ⧖ ⧖

In the first year of King Cyrus of Persia the LORD stirred the heart of Cyrus to put this proclamation in writing and to send it throughout his kingdom:

'The God of heaven has given me all the kingdoms of the earth. He has appointed me to build him a Temple at Jerusalem, which is in Judah. Any of you who are his people may go there for this task. And may the LORD your God be with you!'

Then God stirred the hearts of the leaders of Judah to go to Jerusalem to rebuild the Temple. A total of 42,360 people returned to Judah. When they arrived, the priests and some of the common people settled in villages near Jerusalem. The rest of the people returned to their own towns throughout Israel.

The construction of the Temple began during the second year after they arrived in Jerusalem, and when the builders completed the work, the Temple was dedicated with great joy by the people who had returned from exile.

Many years later, a man named Ezra, a scribe who was well versed in the Law of Moses, came up to Jerusalem from Babylon. The people asked Ezra to bring out the Book of the Law of Moses. So Ezra brought the Book before the assembly, and read aloud to everyone who could understand. All the people listened closely.

Then Ezra praised the LORD, and all the people chanted, 'Amen! Amen!'

Epilogue: A prophecy

(Isaiah 40.1–8)

'Comfort, comfort my people,' says your God.
'Speak tenderly to Jerusalem.
Tell her that her sad days are gone
   and her sins are pardoned.'

Listen! It's the voice of someone shouting,
'Clear the way through the wilderness
   for the LORD!
Make a straight highway through the wasteland
   for our God!
Fill in the valleys,
   and level the mountains and hills.
Straighten the curves,
   and smooth out the rough places.
Then the glory of the LORD will be revealed,
   and all people will see it together.'

A voice said, 'Shout!'
   I asked, 'What should I shout?'

'Shout that people are like the grass.
    Their beauty fades as quickly
    as the flowers in a field.
The grass withers and the flowers fade
    beneath the breath of the Lord.
    And so it is with people.
The grass withers and the flowers fade,
    but the word of our God stands for ever.'

PART 2

SCENES FROM THE NEW TESTAMENT

Prologue: In the beginning

In the beginning the Word already existed.
The Word was with God, and the Word was God.
    He existed in the beginning with God.

The Word gave life to everything that was created,
    and his life brought light to everyone.

The light shines in the darkness,
    and the darkness can never extinguish it.

The Word became human and made his home
        among us.
    He was full of unfailing love and faithfulness.

14

Jesus is born

God sent the angel Gabriel to Nazareth, a village in Galilee, to a virgin named Mary. She was engaged to be married to a man named Joseph, a descendant of King David. Gabriel appeared to her and said,

> 'Don't be afraid, Mary, for you have found favour
> with God! You will conceive and give birth to a son,
> and you will name him Jesus. He will be called the
> Son of the Most High. And his Kingdom will never
> end!'

Mary responded, 'I am the Lord's servant. May everything you have said about me come true.'

At that time the Roman emperor, Augustus, decreed that a census should be taken throughout the Empire. And because Joseph was a descendant of King David, he had to go to Bethlehem in Judea, David's ancient home. He took with him Mary, to whom he was engaged, who was now expecting a child.

While they were there, she gave birth to her first-born son. She wrapped him snugly in strips of cloth and laid him in a manger, because there was no lodging available for them.

That night there were shepherds in the fields nearby, guarding their sheep. Suddenly, an angel of the Lord appeared among them, and the radiance of the Lord's glory surrounded them. 'Don't be afraid!' he said.

'I bring you good news. The Saviour – yes, the Messiah – has been born today in Bethlehem!'

Suddenly, the angel was joined by a vast host of others, praising God and saying,

'Glory to God in highest heaven,
and peace on earth to those with whom
God is pleased.'

When the angels had returned to heaven, the shepherds hurried to the village and found Mary and Joseph. And there was the baby, lying in the manger.

Jesus was born during the reign of King Herod. About that time some wise men from eastern lands arrived in Jerusalem, asking, 'Where is the newborn king of the Jews? We saw his star as it rose, and we have come to worship him.'

King Herod was deeply disturbed when he heard this. He told them, 'Go and search carefully for the child. And when you find him, come back and tell me so that I can go and worship him, too!'

After this the wise men went their way. And the star they had seen in the east guided them to the place where the child was. They entered the house and saw the child with his mother, Mary, and they worshipped him. Then they opened their treasure chests and gave him gifts of gold, frankincense, and myrrh.

When it was time to leave, they returned to their own country by another route, for God had warned them in a dream not to return to Herod.

After the wise men had gone, an angel of the Lord appeared to Joseph in a dream. 'Get up! Flee to Egypt with the child and his mother,' the angel said, 'because Herod is going to search for the child to kill him.'

That night Joseph left for Egypt with the child and his mother, and they stayed there until Herod's death.

Herod was furious when he realized that the wise men had outwitted him. He sent soldiers to kill all the boys in and around Bethlehem who were two years old and under.

When Herod died, an angel of the Lord appeared in a dream to Joseph in Egypt. 'Get up!' the angel said. 'Take the child and his mother back to the land of Israel.' So the family returned home to Nazareth. There the child grew up healthy and strong. He was filled with wisdom, and God's favour was on him.

15

The healer

It was the fifteenth year of the reign of Tiberius, the Roman emperor. Pontius Pilate was governor over Judea.

In those days John the Baptist came to the Judean wilderness and began preaching. The prophet Isaiah was speaking about John when he said,

> 'He is a voice shouting in the wilderness,
>> "Prepare the way for the Lord's coming!"'

Then Jesus went from Galilee to the River Jordan to be baptized by John. As Jesus came up out of the water, the heavens were opened and he saw the Spirit of God descending like a dove and settling on him. And a voice from heaven said, 'This is my dearly loved Son, who brings me great joy.'

Jesus was about thirty years old when he was led by the Spirit in the wilderness, where he was tempted by the devil for forty days. Jesus ate nothing all that time and became very hungry. Then the devil said to him, 'If you are the Son of God, tell this stone to become a loaf of bread.'

But Jesus told him, 'No! The Scriptures say, "People do not live by bread alone."'

Then Jesus returned to Galilee. When he came to Nazareth, his boyhood home, he went as usual to the synagogue on the Sabbath and stood up to read the Scriptures.

The scroll of Isaiah the prophet was handed to him. He unrolled the scroll and found the place where this was written:

'The Spirit of the Lord is upon me,
    for he has anointed me to bring Good News to
        the poor.
He has sent me to proclaim that captives will be
    released,
    that the blind will see,
that the oppressed will be set free,
    and that the time of the Lord's favour has come.'

He rolled up the scroll and sat down. All eyes in the synagogue looked at him intently. Then he began to speak to them. 'The Scripture you've just heard has been fulfilled this very day!'

Then Jesus went to Capernaum, a town in Galilee. Once when he was in the synagogue, a man possessed by an evil spirit cried out, shouting, 'Go away, Jesus of Nazareth! I know who you are – the Holy One of God!'

But Jesus reprimanded him. 'Be quiet! Come out of the man,' he ordered. At that, the demon threw the man to the floor; then it came out of him without hurting him further.

Amazed, the people exclaimed, 'What authority and power this man's words possess! Even evil spirits obey him!'

As the sun went down that evening, people throughout the village brought sick family members to Jesus. No matter what their diseases were, the touch of his hand healed every one.

Early the next morning Jesus went out to an isolated place. The crowds searched everywhere for him, and when they finally found him, they begged him not to leave. But he replied, 'I must preach the Good News of the Kingdom of God in other towns, too, because that is why I was sent.'

So he continued to travel around, preaching in synagogues throughout Judea.

When Jesus returned to Capernaum, a Roman officer came and pleaded with him, 'Lord, my young servant lies in bed, paralysed and in terrible pain.'

Jesus said, 'I will come and heal him.'

But the officer said, 'Lord, I am not worthy to have you come into my home. Just say the word from where you are, and my servant will be healed.'

When Jesus heard this, he was amazed. Turning to those who were following him, he said,

'I tell you the truth, I haven't seen faith like this in all Israel! And I tell you this, that many Gentiles will come from all over the world and sit down with Abraham, Isaac, and Jacob in the Kingdom of Heaven. But many Israelites – those for whom the

Kingdom was prepared – will be thrown into outer darkness.'

Then Jesus said to the Roman officer, 'Go back home. Because you believed, it has happened.' And the young servant was healed that same hour.

One Sabbath day as Jesus was teaching in a synagogue, he saw a woman who had been crippled for eighteen years and was unable to stand up straight.

When Jesus saw her, he called her over and said, 'Dear woman, you are healed of your sickness!' Then he touched her, and instantly she could stand straight.

But the leader in charge of the synagogue was indignant that Jesus had healed her on the Sabbath day. 'There are six days of the week for working,' he said to the crowd. 'Come on those days to be healed, not on the Sabbath.'

But the Lord replied, 'You hypocrites! Each of you works on the Sabbath day! Don't you untie your ox or your donkey from its stall on the Sabbath and lead it out for water? This dear woman, a daughter of Abraham, has been held in bondage by Satan for eighteen years. Isn't it right that she be released, even on the Sabbath?'

This shamed his enemies, but all the people rejoiced at the wonderful things he did.

As Jesus was walking along, he saw a man named Matthew sitting at his tax collector's booth. 'Follow me and be my disciple,' Jesus said to him. So Matthew got up and followed him.

Later, Matthew invited Jesus and his disciples to his

home as dinner guests, along with many tax collectors and other disreputable sinners. But when the Pharisees saw this, they asked his disciples, 'Why does your teacher eat with such scum?'

When Jesus heard this, he said, 'Healthy people don't need a doctor – sick people do.' Then he added,

'Now go and learn the meaning of this Scripture:
"I want you to show mercy, not offer sacrifices." For
I have come to call not those who think they are
righteous, but those who know they are sinners.'

One day soon afterwards Jesus went up on a mountain, and he prayed to God all night. At daybreak he called together all of his disciples and chose twelve of them to be apostles. Here are their names:

Simon (whom he named Peter),
Andrew (Peter's brother),
James,
John,
Philip,
Bartholomew,
Matthew,
Thomas,
James (son of Alphaeus),
Simon (who was called the zealot),
Judas (son of James),
Judas Iscariot.

One day Jesus left the crowds to pray alone. Only his disciples were with him, and he asked them, 'Who do people say I am?'

'Well,' they replied, 'some say John the Baptist, some say Elijah, and others say you are one of the other ancient prophets risen from the dead.'

Then he asked them, 'But who do you say I am?' Peter replied, 'You are the Messiah sent from God!'

Later, Jesus took Peter, James, and John, and led them up a high mountain to be alone. As the men watched, Jesus' appearance was transformed, and his clothes became dazzling white. Then Elijah and Moses appeared and began talking with Jesus.

Then a cloud overshadowed them, and a voice from the cloud said, 'This is my dearly loved Son. Listen to him.' Suddenly, when they looked around, Moses and Elijah were gone, and they saw only Jesus.

16

The teacher

One day as he saw the crowds gathering, Jesus went up on the mountainside and sat down. His disciples gathered around him, and he began to teach them.

> 'God blesses those who are poor and realize their
>   need for him,
>   for the Kingdom of Heaven is theirs.
> God blesses those who mourn,
>   for they will be comforted.
> God blesses those who are humble,
>   for they will inherit the whole earth.
> God blesses those who hunger and thirst for justice,
>   for they will be satisfied.
> God blesses those who are merciful,
>   for they will be shown mercy.
> God blesses those whose hearts are pure,
>   for they will see God.
> God blesses those who work for peace,
>   for they will be called the children of God.
> God blesses those who are persecuted for doing right,
>   for the Kingdom of Heaven is theirs.

'To you who are willing to listen, I say:
Love your enemies!
  Do good to those who hate you.
Bless those who curse you.
  Pray for those who hurt you.
If someone slaps you on one cheek,
  offer the other cheek also.
If someone demands your coat,
  offer your shirt also.
Give to anyone who asks;
  and when things are taken away from you,
  don't try to get them back.

'Do to others as you would like them to do to you.

'If you love only those who love you,
why should you get credit for that?
  Even sinners love those who love them!
And if you do good only to those who do good to you,
why should you get credit?
  Even sinners do that much!

'Love your enemies!
  Do good to them.
  Lend to them without expecting to be repaid.
Then you will truly be acting as children of the
    Most High,
    for he is kind to those who are unthankful and
    wicked.

'You must be compassionate, just as your Father is
compassionate.

'Do not judge others, and you will not be judged.
   Do not condemn others, or it will all come back
      against you.
Forgive others, and you will be forgiven.
   Give, and you will receive.'

8888

As the time drew near for him to ascend to heaven, Jesus
resolutely set out for Jerusalem.

One day an expert in religious law stood up to test Jesus
by asking him: 'Teacher, what should I do to inherit eternal life?'

Jesus replied, 'What does the law of Moses say?'

The man answered, '"You must love the Lord your God
with all your heart, all your soul, all your strength, and
all your mind." And, "Love your neighbour as yourself."'

'Right!' Jesus told him. 'Do this and you will live!'

The man wanted to justify his actions, so he asked
Jesus, 'And who is my neighbour?'

Jesus replied with a story:

'A Jewish man was travelling from Jerusalem down
to Jericho, and he was attacked by bandits. They
stripped him of his clothes, beat him up, and left
him half dead beside the road.

'By chance a priest came along. But when he saw the man lying there, he crossed to the other side of the road and passed him by. A Temple assistant walked over and looked at him lying there, but he also passed by on the other side.

'Then a despised Samaritan came along, and when he saw the man, he felt compassion for him. Going over to him, the Samaritan soothed his wounds with olive oil and wine and bandaged them.

'Then he put the man on his own donkey and took him to an inn, where he took care of him. The next day he handed the innkeeper two silver coins, telling him, "Look after this man. If his bill runs higher than this, I'll pay you the next time I'm here."

'Now which of these three would you say was a neighbour to the man who was attacked by bandits?' Jesus asked.

The man replied, 'The one who showed him mercy.'

Then Jesus said, 'Yes, now go and do the same.'

Once Jesus was in a certain place, praying. As he finished, one of his disciples came to him and said, 'Lord, teach us to pray.'

Jesus said, 'This is how you should pray:

'Father, may your name be kept holy.
    May your Kingdom come soon.

Give us each day the food we need,
    and forgive us our sins,
        as we forgive those who sin against us.
And don't let us yield to temptation.'

One day some Pharisees and teachers of religious law arrived from Jerusalem to see Jesus. They noticed that some of his disciples failed to follow the Jewish ritual of hand washing before eating.

So the Pharisees asked him, 'Why don't your disciples perform the hand-washing ceremony?'

Then Jesus called to the crowd to come and hear. 'All of you listen,' he said, 'and try to understand. It's not what goes into your body that defiles you; you are defiled by what comes from your heart.' (By saying this, he declared that every kind of food is acceptable in God's eyes.)

And then he added,

'For from within, out of a person's heart, come evil thoughts, sexual immorality, theft, murder, adultery, greed, wickedness, deceit, lustful desires, envy, slander, pride, and foolishness. All these vile things come from within; they are what defile you.'

When the Pharisees heard his reply, they met together to question him again.

One of them, an expert in religious law, tried to trap him with this question: 'Teacher, which is the most important commandment in the law of Moses?'

Jesus replied,

> '"You must love the Lord your God with all your
> heart, all your soul, and all your mind." This is
> the first and greatest commandment. A second is
> equally important: "Love your neighbour as your-
> self." The entire law and all the demands of the
> prophets are based on these two commandments.'

The next morning he was at the Temple. A crowd gathered,
and he sat down and taught them. As he was speaking,
the teachers of religious law and the Pharisees brought a
woman who had been caught in the act of adultery. They
put her in front of the crowd.

'Teacher,' they said to Jesus, 'this woman was caught
in the act of adultery. The law of Moses says to stone her.
What do you say?'

They were trying to trap him into saying something
they could use against him. They kept demanding an
answer, so he stood up and said, 'Let the one who has
never sinned throw the first stone!'

When the accusers heard this, they slipped away one
by one, until only Jesus was left in the middle of the crowd
with the woman.

Then Jesus said to the woman, 'Where are your accusers? Didn't even one of them condemn you?'

'No, Lord,' she said.

And Jesus said, 'Neither do I. Go and sin no more.'

The next day, a large crowd of Passover visitors took

palm branches and went down the road to meet him. They shouted, 'Praise God! Blessings on the one who comes in the name of the Lord! Hail to the King of Israel!'

Then Jesus entered the Temple and began to drive out the people selling animals for sacrifices. He said to them, 'The Scriptures declare, "My Temple will be a house of prayer," but you have turned it into a den of thieves.'

After that, he taught daily in the Temple, but the leading priests and the other leaders began planning how to kill him.

Then Judas Iscariot, one of the twelve disciples, went to the leading priests and captains of the Temple guard to discuss the best way to betray Jesus to them.

17

The sacrifice

On the first day of the Festival of Unleavened Bread, when the Passover lamb is sacrificed, Jesus sent two disciples into the city, and they prepared the Passover meal there.

In the evening Jesus arrived with the Twelve. As they were eating, Jesus took some bread and blessed it. Then he broke it in pieces and gave it to the disciples, saying, 'Take it, for this is my body.'

And he took a cup of wine and said to them, 'This is my blood, which confirms the covenant between God and his people. It is poured out as a sacrifice for many.'

Then he got up from the table, and poured water into a basin to wash the disciples' feet. After, he asked,

'Do you understand what I was doing? I have given you an example to follow. Love each other in the same way I have loved you. There is no greater love than to lay down one's life for one's friends.'

Then they sang a hymn and went out to the Mount of Olives.

On the way, Jesus told them, 'All of you will desert me.'

Peter said to him, 'I never will.'

Jesus replied, 'I tell you the truth, Peter – this very night, before the cock crows, you will deny that you even know me.'

They went to the olive grove called Gethsemane, and Jesus said, 'My soul is crushed with grief to the point of death. Stay here and keep watch with me.'

He went on a little further and fell to the ground. 'Abba, Father,' he cried out, 'please take this cup of suffering away from me. Yet I want your will to be done, not mine.'

Then he returned and found the disciples asleep. He said to Peter, 'Keep watch and pray. For the spirit is willing, but the body is weak.'

As Jesus said this, Judas arrived with a crowd of men armed with swords and arrested him.

All his disciples deserted him and ran away.

They took Jesus to the high priest's home. Inside, the leading priests and the entire high council were trying to find evidence against Jesus, so they could put him to death. Then the high priest stood up and asked Jesus, 'Are you the Messiah, the Son of the Blessed One?'

Jesus said, 'I Am.'

Then the high priest tore his clothing and said, 'You have all heard his blasphemy. What is your verdict?'

'Guilty!' they all cried. 'He deserves to die!'

Then some of them began to spit at him and beat him.

Meanwhile, Peter was in the courtyard below. One of the servant girls who worked for the high priest noticed

Peter. She looked at him closely and said, 'You were one of those with Jesus of Nazareth.'

But Peter denied it. 'I don't know what you're talking about,' he said. Just then, a cock crowed. Suddenly, Jesus' words flashed through Peter's mind. And he broke down and wept.

Then the entire council took Jesus to Pilate, the Roman governor. They began to state their case: 'This man has been leading our people astray by claiming he is the Messiah, a king.'

So Pilate asked him, 'Are you the king of the Jews?'

Jesus answered, 'My Kingdom is not an earthly kingdom.'

Pilate said, 'So you are a king?'

Jesus responded, 'I came into the world to testify to the truth.'

'What is truth?' Pilate asked.

Then Pilate had Jesus flogged with a lead-tipped whip. The soldiers wove a crown of thorns and put it on his head, and they put a purple robe on him. 'Hail! King of the Jews!' they mocked.

Pilate went outside again and said to the people, 'I am going to bring him out to you now, but understand clearly that I find him not guilty.'

Then Jesus came out wearing the crown of thorns and the purple robe. And Pilate said, 'Look, here is the man!'

When they saw him, the leading priests and Temple guards began shouting, 'Crucify him! Crucify him!'

Pilate saw that he wasn't getting anywhere and that a

riot was developing. So he sent for a bowl of water and washed his hands before the crowd, saying, 'I am innocent of this man's blood. The responsibility is yours!'

Then they led him away to be crucified.

Two others, both criminals, were led out to be executed with him. When they came to a place called The Skull, they nailed him to the cross. And Jesus said, 'Father, forgive them, for they don't know what they are doing.'

At midday, darkness fell across the whole land until three o'clock. At about three o'clock, Jesus called out with a loud voice, 'My God, my God, why have you abandoned me?'

Suddenly, the curtain in the sanctuary of the Temple was torn down the middle. Then Jesus shouted, 'Father, I entrust my spirit into your hands!' And with those words he breathed his last.

When the Roman officer who stood facing him saw how he had died, he exclaimed, 'This man truly was the Son of God!'

Some women were there, watching from a distance, including Mary Magdalene. They had been followers of Jesus and had cared for him while he was in Galilee.

As his body was taken away, the women followed and saw the tomb where his body was placed. Then they went home and prepared spices and ointments to anoint his body.

Early on Sunday morning, while it was still dark, Mary Magdalene came to the tomb and found that the stone had been rolled away from the entrance.

Mary was standing outside the tomb crying, and as she wept, she stooped and looked in. She saw two white-robed angels, one sitting at the head and the other at the foot of the place where the body of Jesus had been lying.

'Dear woman, why are you crying?' the angels asked her.

'Because they have taken away my Lord,' she replied, 'and I don't know where they have put him.'

She turned to leave and saw someone standing there. It was Jesus, but she didn't recognize him.

'Dear woman, why are you crying?' Jesus asked her. 'Who are you looking for?'

She thought he was the gardener.

'Sir,' she said, 'if you have taken him away, tell me where you have put him, and I will go and get him.'

'Mary!' Jesus said.

She turned to him and cried out, 'Teacher!'

'Don't cling to me,' Jesus said, 'but go and find my brothers and tell them, "I am ascending to my Father and your Father, to my God and your God."'

Mary Magdalene found the disciples and told them, 'I have seen the Lord!'

That evening the disciples were meeting behind locked doors because they were afraid of the Jewish leaders.

Suddenly, Jesus was standing there among them!

'Peace be with you,' he said.

18

Acts of the apostles

During the forty days after he suffered and died, Jesus appeared to the apostles, and he talked to them about the Kingdom of God.

They kept asking him, 'Lord, has the time come for you to free Israel and restore our kingdom?'

He replied,

> 'The Father alone has the authority to set those dates and times, and they are not for you to know. But you will receive power when the Holy Spirit comes upon you. And you will be my witnesses, to the ends of the earth.'

After saying this, he was taken up into a cloud, and they could no longer see him.

On the day of Pentecost all the believers were in one place. Suddenly, there was a sound from heaven like the roaring of a mighty windstorm. Everyone present was filled with the Holy Spirit and began speaking in other languages.

At that time there were devout Jews from every nation

living in Jerusalem. When they heard the loud noise, everyone stood there amazed and perplexed.

Then Peter stepped forward and shouted to the crowd, 'Listen carefully, all of you! What you see was predicted long ago by the prophet Joel:

"In the last days," God says, "I will pour out my Spirit upon all people – men and women alike – and they will prophesy."

'People of Israel, listen! God publicly endorsed Jesus by doing powerful miracles through him. But with the help of lawless Gentiles, you nailed him to a cross and killed him. But God raised Jesus from the dead, and we are all witnesses of this.'

Those who believed what Peter said were baptized and all the believers devoted themselves to the apostles' teaching, and to prayer.

8 8 8 8

Stephen, a man full of God's grace and power, performed amazing miracles among the people. But one day men from the synagogue persuaded some others to lie about Stephen, saying,

'This man is always speaking against the holy Temple. We have heard him say that this Jesus of

Nazareth will destroy the Temple and change the customs Moses handed down to us.'

So they arrested Stephen and dragged him out of the city and began to stone him. His accusers took off their coats and laid them at the feet of a young man named Saul.

A great wave of persecution began that day, sweeping over the church in Jerusalem. Saul was going from house to house, dragging out both men and women to throw them into prison.

He went to the high priest. He requested letters addressed to the synagogues in Damascus, asking for their cooperation in the arrest of any followers of the Way he found there.

As he was approaching Damascus, a light from heaven suddenly shone down around him. He fell to the ground and heard a voice saying to him, 'Saul! Saul! Why are you persecuting me?'

'Who are you, lord?' Saul asked.

And the voice replied, 'I am Jesus, the one you are persecuting! Now get up and go into the city, and you will be told what you must do.'

Saul picked himself up, but when he opened his eyes he was blind. So his companions led him by the hand to Damascus, and immediately he began preaching about Jesus in the synagogues, saying, 'He is indeed the Son of God!'

Saul, also known as Paul, and his companions left by ship for Pamphylia. On the Sabbath they went to the synagogue. After the usual readings from the books of Moses and the prophets, Paul started speaking. 'Men of Israel,' he said, 'and you God-fearing Gentiles, listen to me.

'It is one of King David's descendants, Jesus, who is God's promised Saviour of Israel! The people in Jerusalem and their leaders did not recognize Jesus as the one the prophets had spoken about. Instead, they condemned him.

'But God raised him from the dead! And over a period of many days he appeared to those who had gone with him from Galilee to Jerusalem. They are now his witnesses to the people of Israel.

'And now we are here to proclaim that through this man Jesus there is forgiveness for your sins. Everyone who believes in him is made right in God's sight.'

The following week almost the entire city turned out to hear them preach. But when some of the Jews saw the crowds, they slandered Paul and argued against whatever he said.

Then Paul declared, 'It was necessary that we first preach the word of God to you Jews. But since you have rejected it, we will offer it to the Gentiles.'

When the Gentiles heard this, they were very glad and thanked the Lord for his message.

Those escorting Paul went with him to Athens. He was deeply troubled by all the idols he saw. So Paul, standing before the council, addressed them as follows:

'Men of Athens, I notice that you are very religious in every way, for as I was walking along I saw your many shrines. And one of your altars had this inscription on it: "To an Unknown God". This God, whom you worship without knowing, is the one I'm telling you about.

'He is the God who made the world and everything in it. Since he is Lord of heaven and earth, he doesn't live in man-made temples, and human hands can't serve his needs – for he has no needs. He himself gives life and breath to everything.

'His purpose was for the nations to seek after God and perhaps feel their way towards him and find him – though he is not far from any one of us. For in him we live and move and exist.

'God overlooked people's ignorance about these things in earlier times, but now he commands everyone everywhere to repent of their sins and turn to him. For he has set a day for judging the world with justice by the man he has appointed, and he proved to everyone who this is by raising him from the dead.'

When they heard Paul speak about the resurrection, some laughed in contempt, but some joined him and became believers.

Epilogue: A vision

This is a revelation from Jesus Christ.

I saw an angel coming down from heaven with a heavy chain in his hand. He seized that old serpent, who is the devil, and bound him in chains for a thousand years.

And I saw the dead standing before God's throne. Books were opened, including the Book of Life. And the dead were judged according to their deeds.

Then I saw a new heaven and a new earth, for the old heaven and the old earth had disappeared. And I saw the holy city, the new Jerusalem, coming down from God out of heaven like a bride beautifully dressed for her husband.

I heard a loud shout from the throne, saying,

'Look, God's home is now among his people! He will wipe every tear from their eyes, and there will be no more death or sorrow or crying or pain. All these things are gone for ever.'

I saw no temple in the city, and the city has no need of sun or moon, for the glory of God illuminates the city. The nations will walk in its light, and its gates will never be closed.

Then the angel showed me a river, clear as crystal, flowing from the throne of God. On each side of the river grew a tree of life, bearing twelve crops of fruit. The leaves were used for medicine to heal the nations.

'Look, I am coming soon.

'I am the Alpha and the Omega, the First and the Last, the Beginning and the End.

'I, Jesus, give you this message for the churches.'

The Spirit and the bride say, 'Come.'

Amen! Come, Lord Jesus!

May the grace of the Lord Jesus be with God's holy people.

☷ ☷ ☷ ☷

Further reading

The text of *The One Hour Bible* is drawn from the *Holy Bible, New Living Translation* (Anglicized edition, SPCK, 2018).

The NLT is an authoritative version of the Bible rendered faithfully into today's English by an international team of over 90 leading biblical scholars.

For information on the different formats available, visit <www.spckpublishing.co.uk>.

⧗⧗⧗⧗

The following are some introductory books on the Bible published by SPCK. To find out more about any of them, visit <www.spckpublishing.co.uk>.

Beckett, Sister Wendy, *Sister Wendy's Bible Treasury: Stories and Wisdom through the Eyes of Great Painters* (2012).

Beitzel, Barry J., *The SPCK Bible Atlas: The Events, People and Places of the Bible from Genesis to Revelation* (2013).

Burridge, Richard A., *Four Gospels, One Jesus? A Symbolic Reading* (2013).

Dell, Katharine, *Who Needs the Old Testament? Its Enduring Appeal and Why the New Atheists Don't Get it* (2017).

Graystone, Peter, *The Bare Bible: Uncovering the Bible for the First Time (or the Hundredth)* (2018).

Law, Philip, *Praying with the Bible* (2007).

Page, Nick, *The Tabloid Bible* (2016).

Wansbrough, Henry, *The SPCK Bible Guide: An Illustrated Survey of all the Books of the Bible – their Contents, Themes and Teachings* (2013).

Ward, Keith, *What the Bible Really Teaches* (2004).

Wright, Tom, *Why Read the Bible?* (2015).

Timeline and index

Note: All dates are approximate (and in some cases highly debatable).

Timeline and index

Timeline and index

Berlin selon ses envies 143

Les plus belles balades

Envie de...

Carnet pratique 173

Notre sélection de lieux et d'adresses

⊙ Voir

❌ Se restaurer

🍷 Prendre un verre

☆ Sortir

🔒 Shopping

Légende des symboles

📞 Numéro de téléphone
🕐 Horaires d'ouverture
P Parking
🚭 Non-fumeurs
@ Accès Internet
📶 Wi-Fi
🥗 Végétarien
📖 Menu en anglais

👨‍👧 Familles bienvenues
🐾 Animaux acceptés
🚌 Bus
⛴ Ferry
Ⓜ Métro
S Subway
🚊 Tramway
🚆 Train

**Retrouvez facilement chaque adresse
sur les plans de quartiers**

Kimchi Princess

7 ❌ Plan p. 90, C3

Si vous n'avez jamais mang
choisissez cette adresse po
On y sert des classiques co
m (riz, légumes, vi:
la plupart des c
lades cuites de
es de délicieu:
Pour les amat
63 458 0203 ; w
r Strasse 36 ; plats
-Bahn Görlitzer Bahn

Berlin
En quelques jours

Les guides En quelques jours édités par Lonely Planet sont conçus pour vous amener au cœur d'une ville.

Vous y trouverez tous les sites à ne pas manquer, ainsi que des conseils pour profiter de chacune de vos visites. Nous avons divisé la ville en quartiers, accompagnés de plans clairs pour un repérage facile. Nos auteurs expérimentés ont déniché les meilleures adresses dans chaque ville : restaurants, boutiques, bars et clubs... Et pour aller plus loin, découvrez les endroits les plus insolites et authentiques de la capitale allemande dans les pages "100% berlinois".

Ce guide contient également tous les conseils pratiques pour éviter les casse-têtes : itinéraires pour visites courtes, moyens de transport, montant des pourboires, etc.

Grâce à toutes ces infos, soyez sûr de passer un séjour mémorable.

Notre engagement

Les auteurs Lonely Planet visitent en personne, pour chaque édition, les lieux dont ils s'appliquent à faire un compte-rendu précis. Ils ne bénéficient en aucun cas de rétribution ou de réduction de prix en échange de leurs commentaires.